# DIVORCED BUSINESS PARTNERS

# DIVORCED BUSINESS PARTNERS

*a love story*

## EMILY HYLAND

2024 Poetry Prize Winner

HOWLING
BIRD
PRESS

Howling Bird Press
Augsburg University
219 Memorial Hall
Minneapolis, MN 55454

http://engage.augsburg.edu/howlingbird/

Published 2024 by Howling Bird Press
Printed in the United States of America
Cover design by Phyrne Nelson
Typesetting by Nayt Rundquist
This book is set in Kepler Std, Letter Gothic Std & Helvetica

*Divorced Business Partners* book team: Chilah Brown, Pamela Morgan, Phyrne Nelson, Alison Summer, Brent Weaver

This is a work of fiction. Names, characters, businesses, places, events, and incidents in this book are either the product of the author's imagination or used in a fictitious manner. Any resemblance to actual persons, living or dead, or actual events is purely coincidental.

First edition

ISBN: 978-1-7365777-7-6 (paperback)
ISBN: 978-1-7365777-8-3 (ebook)

This book is printed on acid-free paper.

For M

*Time has a way of throwing it all in your face*
*The past, she is haunted, the future is laced*

—Gregory Alan Isakov

*You must know that I do not love you and that I love you,*
*because everything alive has its two sides;*
*a word is one wing of the silence,*
*fire has its cold half*

—Pablo Neruda (translated by Stephen Tapscott)

# CONTENTS

# DIVORCED BUSINESS PARTNERS

# PROLOGUE: BREAKFAST DATE WITH MY EX-HUSBAND

I'm the first to arrive. I didn't mean to be, not that silliness like that matters now. Once in a while, we'll eat a meal together when we're in the same city.

Too much fractured too quickly. Yet when it all passed, somehow there were undamaged pieces, and they rebonded—some vestigial thing lost now seems to fuse us as a sort of kin.

I'd planned to walk in a few minutes late with my sunglasses on. Instead, I time the entrance wrong and catch this seat by the window ten minutes ahead.

The waiter asks, *Would you like something to drink while you wait? A latte? Some chai?*

The best part of breakfast is a warm drink with milk.

*Coffee, please.*

*Cream?*

*Oh, I'm sorry, I didn't realize my sunglasses were still on.* I pull them off to meet the indoor greeting of his kind eyes. *Cream is great,* I smile.

*I figured you were a movie star,* he says and winks and smiles.

Brad arrives in a flannel shirt that doesn't suit his preppy roots. As he walks in, I pick up my book so he sees me reading poetry, just like he left me.

I'm reading about mourning a mother, and I realize I've fixed my coffee just like Mom—rigorously shook the sugar shaker, drowned the coffee in cream, and stirred clockwise around the mug.

I don't look up as I notice him see me, as I notice him walk to the table. I'm buried deep in this poem about grief as a snow angel when he taps me on the shoulder.

*Hey,* he's come to my side of the table presumably thinking I'll stand for a hug.

I fold my book and look up. *Nice shirt.*

1

He sits down. Says something self-deprecating about only buying hipster flannel. He's very thirsty. His upper lip is chapped and he jumps right in talking about the thin air and acclimating to the altitude. I tell him to stop at Whole Foods for ChlorOxygen on the way back to his Airbnb.

The waiter returns. My ex-husband gets some emblematic Christmas-style chile eggs with extra chorizo on the side. As always, he orders *unsweetened iced tea with just a little bit of ice.*

The waiter looks my way. I say, *The avocado toast with poached eggs, please,* grinning widely, *that's the movie star order, right?*

*That's right,* the waiter smiles right back.

*What was that?*

*He thought I was a movie star when I came in because I forgot to take off my sunglasses.*

*Oh,* he smiles.

It's the first meal we eat together in years and the first time together where I'm able to not try and memorialize hypothetical situations, not asking things like,

*Do you ever miss spending your days with me?* or *Do you ever regret leaving?* or *What do you think our life would be like now if we were still together?*

which put him up against a wall and he would say something gut-punching like *Sometimes* or *I don't know, Maddy* or *We'd probably have more cats.*

The truth is, we'd probably be eating eggs across from each other in Brooklyn, or maybe in some city like Portland. I don't think he'd be wearing flannel.

He asks how I like it here.

*I love it,* I jump into my camera and start showing him pictures of my home, the flowering plants, the fireplace, the solar lanterns hanging from the front trees.

We talk a little of his cousins and aunts. I tell him Dad's moving to Florida. I talk about the wedding, I tell him more about Jim, and he tells me about the restaurant he and Serena are trying to open back home.

I'm not jealous he's opening a restaurant with his fiancé.

He doesn't ask about my sister. I don't ask about his son except for a boilerplate, *Gosh, he'll be two already this summer.*

Certain wounds still need tall walls.

When the check comes, he says, *I've got it.*

*Good—I wasn't planning to pay.*

He's still thirsty and it's a nice day, so we head out for a coffee shop around the corner with a short walk on the horizon. At the counter, he says, *I'll be right back.*

I look at the barista and shake my head with tepid chagrin, *I'm stuck paying for my ex-husband's drink, huh?*

What's in the space between both playful and miffed?

Long history. Complicated love and bitterness. Words from the handwritten note I found on his empty dawn pillow—fresh ink: *I can never grow up with someone else again, but this is complacency.*

On pages he ripped from my bedside journal to write that last letter, *It wasn't exciting to kiss someone else, amazing just to feel again.*

I read it just once, then shoved the note into a drawer. Eulogy for a marriage in his summative cursive: *You say no one will love me more. That's true. No one will betray me more either.*

Like I am forced to chew and swallow rocks, these words crack my molars now—years later—just to type.

Nobody tells you about how life winds up so and untangles. Little rope knots the resilient ones understand and then nod with warm and passive smiles that we all go there, we all are here, this is living.

But it didn't feel like living until the fire started, until I was spat out and hot, was the embers, until I was spinning, spinning away from one thing and into another.

I tell the barista, *He'll have an unsweetened iced tea with just a little bit of ice.*

And while I wait there with the drink I'd dropped a compostable pink straw into (I knew he'd want the pink one), I remember the afternoon when I drove upstate to collect a box of my journals from his mother's house: it's spring—the fiddleheads are wild against my shins as I slink up the front walkway and ring the doorbell I've never had to ring before.

*Come in, dear*, I hear his mother say through the thick wood, but I wait until she opens it—not my home to stroll into anymore. Then, as I'm here for this particular task, we head upstairs, and suddenly I'm in his closet: such scenic nearness.

His mother ambles behind me, *Which box are you taking?*

I've had this one box tucked into the corner under streamers of his shirts from high school and his father's blazers of tweed and twill and herringbone too short in the arms but too sweet-smelling of paternal cigars and musk to let go—

I know this wall of ties so well, this stack of children's books, the pack of negatives from his photo class—this back-country home, greenery of high summer, thicket of foresty yard, algae pond, damp must and mold of age and past and dry rot in the wood—I'm transported into his childhood.

There's a set of built-in drawers; I open the top one to peek to see. Still all there: presents from me, picture collage and my honest first poems, poems with lines like,

> out into the starry night I look at you
> I look at love and the moon up above—

I leave them there and carry my package downstairs. His mother asks if I'll stay for dinner.

*I shouldn't.*

*Would you like some iced tea before you go?*

*No thank you, no.*

I put my shoes back on and look into the fold of the home: the gold chairs in the dining room and the landscape above the hearth where my stocking used to hang each year.

*This is the last time I'll ever be in this place.*

*Don't be silly you can come visit anytime.*

It's already been six years since my toes touched those floors and climbed those creaky stairs.

I remember in the early days, when we slept in separate rooms, still college teens, how I'd moonwalk the floorboards from his room back to the guest nook, how much I enjoyed the terrycloth ribs of the comforter under which I'd sleep after creeping from his bed, sneaking away from our love in the darkest hours of the new day.

# HONEYMOON TIDE

We're near shore—the swells
churn into a rogue washer. By the time

I break above the surface, he's already
standing, ankles in the surf—where water

meets earth—waves me in, calling, *The tide
has changed! Swim in, swim in!*

# WHAT I NOTICE

After I notice that the aberrant hair peeking out of Brad's left nostril
might just activate my extra-sensory perception, I have a premonition

on the second floor of Amore, over our cacio e pepe:
I foresee the night at Luke's Inn when our fortune cookie

mini-scrolls will share the same seven numbers. I have faith:
if we play them in Powerball, we'll win and he'll marry me.

That night, I down three Dr. Funks filled with absinthe.
At the gas station where we stop on the way home, I play

the wrong numbers. Later, I dream of the afternoon in Philly
when we sing together in the shower of Brad's Rittenhouse studio.

In the sheen of that water is the first time I notice
the smoothness of the scar on the belly of his bicep—it cuts

like a marlin below the sea's surface. In the morning, my headache
fades as the bang of orgasm shakes me. Unmystically,

I notice the way Brad's cum always looks like a silk-
worm, sluicing downward, running out of me.

# RESTAURANT BUILD-OUT

Not courageous so much as impulsive, we jump into the abyss: cracked
kitchen tiles and equipment barnacled with gunk so thick with grime
and trash, there's no choice but for the family to jump in and help.

That summer into fall, Mom spends whole days attacking rusted metro
shelves with a futile metal scrubby while Dad and I drive to the Lowe's
in Red Hook, then to Ikea, then back again only to find what we bought
was a touch too small or off, or wrong.

So we hop back into the Jeep to curse in chorus down trafficked corridors
of Park Slope, speeding to Home Depot on perpetual treasure hunt for some
obscure bolt or latch or hook so particular only restaurant build-outs seem
to warrant its use.

One afternoon, on a coffee run for the construction crew, Dad asks me,
*Are you sure you want to go into business with your husband? Have you two
thought this through?*

Together twelve years, married for six—*Ugh, we're fine.* What could he know?
*It might put great strain on things,* he says.

*Okay, Dad.*

# WHEN WE OPEN THE RESTAURANT

Success hits hard
alights our heads

with gray. The only way
to hold each other

quickly becomes stolen
hugs in front of the oven.

I want to see my husband again—
creature whose hair is a lullaby

across his face
on the pillow at night.

# ONE NIGHT, EARLY ON

As we're about to leave, Brad pops
into the bathroom to pee before we go.

He comes out with a torn look on his face.
*Are you okay? What's going on?* I ask.

He says, *There's a baby mouse in there
in the corner.* He knows by speaking it

alive, he's assigned its death. So tiny,
nobody would've seen the pink creature

curled into the place where floor meets
wall at the foot of the garbage.

When he escorts me in to see, we stand,
as parents we'll never be together, admiring

the unopened eyes of the newborn as if she
predates her own creation by three years

as a warning in the shape of this little mouse.
If she foreshadowed her own life, neither

of us noticed the omen. The mouse is a pink
eraser; she was a pomegranate seed before

I washed her away. She announced herself
the month after he left. Why would I grow

what had already gone? We contemplate
options in the dim-lit room.

What's the choice? Brad swaddles the mouse
in a kitchen towel. He cups the poor thing

in his palms. If he lets it go free, it won't
survive the cold. He carries mouse, gently,

out to the street. This will be its only time
to breathe fresh air. A moment of life under

stars and wind against its pruney, unfurred skin.
He folds the towel over mouse well and puts

the bundle down. Pauses. The air is winter
clear. He breathes a long breath in, looks up

at the inky sky, then stamps
his heel down hard.

# BRAD AT THE OVEN

The whole room buzzes in chatter
and cheer of a fast-paced service,
servers carry dishes moments out
of the fire, fingertips accustomed
to heat, I tread hours deep in host-
stand-waitlist frenzy—every table
full with diners pouring in, and in
the middle of it, I look down this
certain place in time to where Brad
turns cast irons in the open kitchen—
his forearm hair scorched short—
the whole thing of it centers on his
movements—what's within him—
at the copper-sheathed oven that'll
patina, weathering over a decade.
In the muck, our contact's just about
the chores of it all—more small bills
from the bank, fire inspector punch-
list, more wobble wedges from Chef's
Warehouse, again, more forks.

# THE WINE ROOM

Brad and I kill spiders on our hands and knees, spray and wipe our way through rolls of paper towels until the little room is beholden to our dreams. We paint soft lavender with leftover paint from our bedroom; two plastic chairs and a cheap table serve as our desk. How naive to think so much real estate could be free from storage in that basement? Nowhere to put anything, everything takes over. That table and chairs decamp to a better home. Fridges and wire racks wall the perimeter: asymmetrical, uneven, so I tie string around the wire-rack poles with cardboard fencing at each end so bottles won't fall too often. The wine room is the office and also really neither of either. A few square feet of turf for admin and storage space, it's an offshoot of the dish pit butting up to the walk-in on one side and the boiler room on the other. I sit in the wine room alcove on a wine box seat with a wobbling chair as my desk

to run payroll with noise-cancelers on to concentrate in that space forever cluttered with random parts of the Robot Coupe and KitchenAid. No room for a door—staff takes lots of beer for we've no place to lock the bottles up. The wine room's a type of closet, too, shared by all. Socks and shoes tucked under a rack, umbrella wedged into a corner, forgotten shirt crumpled onto a stack of paperwork sitting atop the printer, an unprinting tombstone to itself. Right now, Brad and I are in the wine room, five feet from our porter Omar, as he lathers and listens to harmonic improvisations on the saxophone through static of cellar a.m. radio waves to avoid listening to the disharmony and ascending volume of our voices. A guest's upset her fusilli didn't have enough mushrooms. She wanted extra mushrooms. A waitress brought the dish back to show Chef Brad her concern. She comes to me, *The guest wants*

*more mushrooms. I don't understand why we can't just add them. Can you please talk to him?* Right now, our voices rise. He hisses, *You're not my teacher! Stop sounding like a teacher!* It's always the same in the heightened midst— I want to talk now; he doesn't. I can't not press; he can't express needs calmly. I devolve into reactivity—he goes mean in response. I need resolution; he needs space. We're terrible with each other in difficult moments. I feel Omar's eyes fixed down on the sink. I plead in louder whisper that's hardly whisper at all, *Keep it down—please. Calm down!* He doesn't want to be calm, doesn't want to negotiate workplace drama with me. Most nights, we leave together once the floor is mopped, walking home and counting rats as they scatter across the late-night streets. Tonight, he'll go without me. I'll take a moment within the cluttered nook, then bolt upstairs. The expo is yelling, *Hands!*

I go back in, *Take this to table three.* I charge back into the barrage.

# NEW ROUTINE

We get the set all ready again:
the tables set, setting up the kitchen, setting the dough

to rest—it becomes a braiding of each day into the next.
More often, we work longer days, and our eyes

don't meet. All we do is go to bed, then wake to toss
on the same combination of wrinkled jeans and tees

and scoot over to the restaurant so he can slice the necks
and legs off ducks and I can arrange boxes of liquor on racks,

replenish the host stand, and sweep the dining room. Then at dinner,
the room comes alive, and we interface expeditiously,

precise. He says, *Apps to table two. Fire table eight. Go with this*,
and I'm away into the ocean of eaters.

One routine afternoon, we set aside a moment for lunch.
I look at him, lock in and wait. I think he sees me,

but a vacancy dwells. He sees me lost in this creature we built
with our hands, our funds, and our family. Now, he sees

we have turned his dream into truth. He stands
at the apogee of his life in meteoric rise,

and he sees in the distance the expanse of sky
and possibilities. I cannot.

# HATCH

Brad and I just had another argument mid-service—
it was horrible, the yelling—

I've come out for air; Joey's taking a break from the line, so I lean against bricks
while Joey chain smokes and ruminates.

He tells me, *You're a beam of light.* He paces in orbit around me,
and each footstep he takes clangs the hatch near the latch.

I can't see stars beyond the fuzzy city mug of gray, but we're aglow in the halo
of streetlamp and car light, tuned into the landscape's hum.

There are these things I want to say. I say, *There's a lot unspoken between us*—
I lean. He continues to patrol this true moment, continues to smoke,

to look at me and then to look away—
we look out beyond the weedy chain link, past cars beeping down the avenue,

then he notices I bite my lip. He tells me, *You bite your lip when you hesitate.*
I know he's right. I also spin my ring with my right thumb and pointer

in hot circles like a race car
burning the pavement around a track.

# WEDDING RINGS & SOURDOUGH

do not go together, no.

We walk to the restaurant, then he slips his ring off to work with his hands—
mixing dampened flour he'll later shape and leave to proof

and he can't risk wearing it then either—it might come off
and bake into a boule, and some diner might choke

so he keeps it off in prep and off in service, too. My fingers notice

it doesn't go back on when I take his hand on the late walk home—
soon it just lives on the nightstand, a reminder: absence in proximity

how we each begin rolling toward our edge—the bedding separates
and holds us, both: he, tangled in the sheet with his toes out

and I, warm in the comforter.

# NEAR THE END

He stays out with her until sunrise, sitting on a knoll
watching jetsam catch moonlight on the river. *We made out,* he tells me later,

*then I threw up and took a car home.*
I've been staying out until the bars close with Joey on Saturdays,

anyway, ripping coasters into sawdust while drinking IPA.
I've been asking him to kiss me, trying to wriggle my hand

into his in an Uber over the bridge back to Brooklyn.
He always keeps the boundary. I don't even realize

how much I want to break my marriage.
A week after Brad leaves, we have to shoot a PR piece.

The director has us stand together, keeps saying, *Closer!*
Then once we're as close as the fiction insists,

he cues me to say, *I love pasta,* then Brad to say, *and I love you*
then for us to look at each other and give the camera a wedding-altar kiss.

The piece doesn't air.

## NOTHING HAS EVER TAKEN HIM FURTHER AWAY
## FROM ME

I thought we'd been through it all—as if untimely
catastrophe would be its own protection: his father

dropping into death overnight, shirt for the next day
draped over the banister and half an iced tea

on the top shelf of the fridge with cubes
still intact for the morning.

It can't have been easy for Brad to have been the one
to commit to the end of our marriage—to call it—

and I'm always still proud of him—like a river
of its smoothest rocks—obsidian and iridescent

in the sunlight like glitter. Years ago, I turned my eyes
to his happy eyes. We held hands and jumped

into the restaurant
like into a speedboat.

When I asked, *What if we fail?*
He said, *We won't.*

# OUT TO DINNER WITH MY HUSBAND WHEN WE ARE SEPARATED

We meet at some fancy city spot set aside for seminal nights
—anniversaries and birthdays alike—but for us what's become

another Tuesday—a place to look across a schism of starched napery
and toile of countless thread, where we watch a taper candle

flicker and dribble in the dread of its own knowing.
We're every part of the rabbit we order on special.

Gutted and cooked, it's unrecognizable as a creature anymore
yet so fucking delicious in its sauce, we slide our fingers

around the sides of our plates, and reach through the thicket
of tableware and tulips of wine—russet, burgundy, blush—

into the wellspring where space has been cleared for our marriage:
to lick the flavor off each other's fingers, wanton and wayward,

and still not able to hold hands upon leaving, or return to a common
home to get out of our clothes—we only share a car back over the bridge.

He gets out first, and I continue on, unable to touch what's aching.

# ASSAULT WITH A ~~WEAPON~~ CANVAS BAG

*Is it true?* I ask him on the street outside the restaurant.
He's moving in with her—

He looks off. Out of focus, a dragonfly zips by.
*Is it true?* He locks in—and when I ask,

*How long has it been?* He says with a dead
arrow, *It's none of your business,*

and there's this moment of space in between
my breath in and my breath out

where I still in the dark ice
of this impossible storyline

as if curled into him watching a plot
unfold like in *Birdman*, then pulling apart

to look at each other, astonished, and ask,
*What just happened?*

I throw a seltzer can at his chest, then shove
him from the sink in my breast—

I don't see red, as they say—
move first as witness to myself

undone in fury, then lose any track
of action. I know I swung

my bag and screamed, I know I kept
trying and trying to wake him back up—

where has he gone—the man
who took my hand across the streets?

The men from the barbershop pour out
to break up the scene, my service team

peeks out from the restaurant window,
lighting candles, and as it goes

two officers are strolling by, so when I sort of
come out of my initial daze,

I stand handcuffed
my stuff strewn across the hatch

I hear the well and wallop of my sounds
somewhere between howls and mourning sobs

I hear the barber urge, *Be calm*
but I can't steady, seeing past to Brad

who does look calm—on his phone—
he stands away, collar still correctly

creased, the white of his shirt
unsullied, untouched—

hair neat. He looks away,
chest steered down the street

toward where she lives,
and he heads out as I'm taken in.

# GOING TO THE BATHROOM IN CENTRAL BOOKING

When the officer walks me into the cell, I see the metal toilet

in the open in the left corner by the bars. It's not even

in the back. There are twelve bars. I try to remember it all—

I count the bars: *twelve bars.* Eighteen other women,

two benches, both taken; the vent amassed with dust,

a lint trap thick. I sit on the floor, gather myself back,

touch my wrists—bruised from the cuffs, remember my body—

the brush of air on my skin. *Oof*—and the pressure of urine

above and behind my pubic bone—

it's now been hours, and I decide to hold it—

*How long can this possibly take?* By now,

someone must've told my sister. Some lawyer

must be on the way. I know there is a lawyer

on the way. The lawyer must be on the way.

The only place to really sit is near the toilet—

the unit is particularly full of tension on this muggy

August afternoon. I need to go. I tell myself,

*We're just a bunch of women sitting on the floor.*

Someone in here has pulled down her pants before—

I'm almost sure. I'm going to have to do this soon

so I might as well do it now, so I ask,

to no one at all, *What do we do when we need to go?*

A cellmate tells me, *Yell to the CO for toilet tissue.*

*She'll bring you some from the roll.*

I thank my friend and press my body to the bars. It feels

unnatural to shout like I would to Mom from the TV

room when she'd call for dinner and we'd call back.

The group is amused by my soft caw out, so someone

hollers—I'm grateful her voice booms and bellows

for me down the hall. The CO gives me a few sheets.

Thank God I only have to pee.

I study the toilet: my complete foe—

see the gunk and crud and film around the seat.

I plan to squat. I take a breath and look around, unbutton

and unzip my jeans, slowly pull the denim down—

and as I start to feel the stream, a fart comes out—

I can't control, it's loud and long, a foghorn blow

that's thick with shame, and on the beat, a peer roars,

*Hot damn this bitch has got some gas!*

Another laughs loud and slaps her leg.

*She could shoot a car across the state!*

The whole cell is rolling on the ground. I wipe so quick,

I feel the wet all down my thigh. I sort of roll my eyes,

then smile too, realize the glue here in this long short spell:

any chance to break the buzz of dwell and hot ennui.

An act of craft—I have more left, so toot again,

and we all crack up so hard it hurts

against the concrete floor

where we'll all together later lay our heads

and wait our turns until we go.

# AFTER DRAFTING THE DIVORCE AGREEMENT

I don't know
how to write

about the way
his eyes look

the last time.

The sparsely
flowered bedding.

It isn't fucking,
it's not *making*

*love,*

it's a powerline
cut, a body alone

in my body, his bile-
eyes above me,

bothered dreamboats

of anger, those eyes
the pitch of raven, star-

less punctures, ink-like
vein popping across

unsunny under eyes,

heavy as if hit.
When it's time to sign,

he makes inane edits
anew. Again,

asks me to dinner.

I want the story to be:
no woman will ever

uncover him more,
will know how his dad

would read to him

at the beach, how
he savored the rustle

of his father's feet
against summer sheets

to lull him to sleep.

And other bits, too:
how he doesn't

like his ribs
to be touched

or the bony part

of his iliac crest—
how to hold him

is a skill of sliding
an arm around

his skein of bones

barely to brush
and be very still.

## ARCHIVAL WORK

In large letters and circled two times around, in black Sharpie, in my journal:

> *The problem is us running a business together—not our relationship!*

& textures of pleading:

> *I'm just asking you to recognize the extraordinary circumstances that have been testing our marriage. I am asking you—with me—to prioritize each other instead of our business.*

We can't.

> *The pressure has fucking destroyed us—that doesn't mean we can't come back together.*

& penned everywhere—Rumi reminds:

> *Gamble everything for love—*

# AFTER MY COURT DATE

We happen upon each other in the dim light of the mustard hall
with speckled floors. He leaves his gloves and pea coat on

as he tells the DA he doesn't want to press charges. Our leaving
aligns; we run up against each other on the sidewalk

then walk a short way together past an old haunt with smoked meat
a few blocks from the courthouse. He gestures me in for some breakfast

then steals away to the bathroom. As the waitress arrives in his absence
I say, *He'll have an unsweetened iced tea with just a little bit of ice.*

He smiles when it arrives, gives me a half-laugh, his once-
wife—we once lived in this world together.

# THE LAST TIME

was the only time
he entered when he
no longer lived at
home. I stood before
the mirror after—
in the bathroom
full of shadows—
I never thought
I'd know something
so wholly, but I'm not
kidding, right there
at the sink—the altar—
I saw my reflection
and knew what rooted
in the strange fertile
ground of my body—
grieving—I couldn't
nurture the despair, so
let go as do trees of
their ambering leaves.

# CELLULAR PARTING

Some clinic Mom finds in midtown: waiting
room, coupled teens in chairs. They call me in

a nurse sticks a thing inside me to confirm.
When it's time, I don't realize—

twilight

barefoot,
stepping on ants in summertime—

red body against red body of patio brick
mushing into naught—

wake up in recovery, choose some crackers.
*I need to pee.* They give me apple juice

and Advil, tell me,
*That's a common sensation.*

# STILL NOT DIVORCED

His marble eyes only gaze past me now. I could wave

my hand up and down in front of his still

face—he wouldn't blink.
                              I choose not to gestate the grief.

        It's different to mourn the living—old ways,

        the crease of the sheets over his napping hips—

# OATH

He gave his word.
Stood with my hands and my eyes
in shared space and placed
a band onto a finger on my hand.
I trusted him like mallards
trust the pond,
yet he flew quick and sharp
like a jab and is gone.

# FRIED BABY ARTICHOKES

I thought I was never
not going to be mad at him.

I look at many recipes,
but I know Brad

can run me through
better than anyone

so I call and I'm right.
Affidavits signed,

we only have to wait
15 to 90 days now.

After Brad details
the steps, I ask,

*How does it feel to finally
be almost divorced?* It's hard—

small talk isn't something
for people mid-post-marriage.

*Is it what you wanted
after all?*

He's just walked into his new
apartment. He's unpacking.

*Maddy, I still have my shoes on.
I don't want to talk about this—*

I get it. No need
for chit-chat

with a stranger
when I know now

how to pan fry the *carciofo*
with precision.

# BURY IT

We should bury it—
that last time together,
the last time—air tough
between us—I sought
anything worth latching
onto, legs akimbo—Brad
pushed with such unex-
pected force of thrust,
life zapped into my body
and grew for weeks, and
for weeks, she grew, until
some doctor dug in to ex-
cavate that little gem, not
buried—dumped instead
into a biohazard bin in the
hallway of medical suite
3125 while Mom waited
for me in a stiff lobby
chair outside.

# RITUAL FOR MY RING

I slide on my wedding ring one last time, then rip
the fabric from our old bedding to wrap the ring,
then seal the clump in a tiny jar. I throw ritual
upon ritual: get a potion from the witch shop

in Bushwick. Wash it over my body. Then,
the ceremonial fucking of another man. A new
Christmas. Tossing poems into the oven.
I bury the ring under earth in a houseplant.

I want to tell you when I dug it up, I cast it
into the ocean then dove into the swells to get it—
no. Even now, I'm pragmatic—find a jeweler
in midtown and sell it. Use the money to pay

the divorce lawyer! Nope. I cross the street
to Aritzia and buy a slinky black dress.

# THE DAY I SIGN THE DIVORCE PAPERS

I hustle without an umbrella through a sudden midsummer downpour
to meet Dad at the attorney's office. When I get there, I sign. Dad scrawls

his name as my witness. After all the fighting and the drafting, the final
strokes to cut our legal bond are quick. After, we get coffee in some corner shop,

then meet Mom to go with her on her rounds at the Perlmutter Cancer Center.
It's a routine affair: bloodwork, checkup, then on to her cubicle for chemo.

It's as mid-August muggy as the city gets; Mom freezes in her green gown.
She pulls a bonnet from her carryall to warm the bald. During check-up,

my mind latches onto certain phrases. *Right mandible . . . pooled with blood . . .*
*swollen . . . occipital ridge . . . pooled.* The doctor palpates her tiny breast,

mostly scar tissue now—nothing suspicious about what's past.
Dr. Breyer says, *The tumor is doing well . . . the fighters are better . . . red cells.*

I recall, *crimson . . . shoals of cells.* Now, she knits while the IV drips.
Yarn wraps around her pointer that shakes in tremor.

We sit in the diner after. She's not supposed to eat anything raw. She orders
a burger rare and laps up the blood like a tiger. Uses a fork for the french fries.

On my walk home, it no longer rains. I step over seven smushed roses, roadside,
their petals give the effect of a blood trail across the crosswalk.

Brad's nicest flowers were his last flowers.

# EUTHANIZING GRAMMY

The vet can only come tonight. I let Brad come over. As soon as he arrives, Grammy settles for her last hours to sleep on his chest.

When it's time, I hold her on my lap while the vet injects sedatives. Then, the poison. Brad wraps his arm around my shoulder, his other hand cupping Grammy's face, which tucks well into his palm.

Years before, we nurse pigeon babies who live in the base of an old plant on the fire escape and feed them cereal from the window until the super realizes and removes them.

Years before that, at the beginning really—in college—I buy Brad an albino leopard Gecko for our anniversary. We name her Rink. On party Saturdays we feed her fresh crickets so everyone stoned can peer into her terrarium for the live-action feasting.

She moves with us from college to that apartment in Brooklyn.

Soon after, we find Rink oddly curled in her water bowl and notice a protrusion from her tail. We don't know what to do, so Brad googles how to euthanize a Gecko at home and learns our options: smash her head with a hammer or tuck her into the freezer.

Freezing is the kindest way. He wraps her in a towel, puts her into the fridge first to put her to sleep, then opens the cold drawer, and slides her in. We bury her the next day on a small hill in Prospect Park.

Tonight, Grammy's limp like a sack of Jell-O. There's no going back.

We stand together in the small apartment after the vet leaves. Alone for the first time in a while, we stand across from the person we wanted to love for the rest of our lives—I see him take my hand.

All I needed those years ago was to hold his hand, but he wouldn't take it.

Now, he says, when I say, *I wanted a different outcome—I wanted one, too.*

Now, he embraces me—tall, ambrosial—the nook of his neck on the right side where my face still fits.

## BABKA

Today, he signs the divorce papers then
sends me our vows in a text,

found them while I was packing —

I bumped into him last weekend
at the restaurant—I noticed he'd brought

fresh babka for the staff, and I couldn't resist,
asked if I could have some.

*Yeah, of course,* he said, *that's why I bought it.*

At the end of the text today, he says,

I hope you are well

# DIVORCED BUSINESS PARTNER MEETING

It's necessary for us to meet to discuss logistics of tables for open-air seating,
and while we're at the restaurant, we taste the new salad: thin slices

of summer squash, shavings of almonds, and yuzu that oils our separate tines
stabbing into a shared bowl. I recently learned it's important to find joy

in the worst things, so I sit kitty-corner to him at the back table after and help
pit high-summer cherries, rubescent and bloody, and our nails bite

into skin—our hands tear, and they plumb flesh as if each
uncovered and tossed pit might lead the way toward something

worth keeping. The aftermath—a horror. Gore lights the table
with piles of ripped-open cherry corpses. Halfway through, we run out

of things to say, and our hands are stained anyway, so we wash them over
and over together in the back kitchen sink that's been missing a leg

since we opened. Water spills into the floor drain, and I wipe the wooden
platter as he sugars, waters, and heats the remainder in some shiny new

saucepan. I'm with the wad of towels soaked garnet
like pantyliners in the days that followed what unraveled

when my body crawled out and out and out of itself.

# DIVORCED BUSINESS PARTNER FAMILY REUNION

Unexpectedly at the restaurant, I see my once-family
again for the first time since our separation.

His cousin has brought her new baby. His mother says, *Hello, dear.*
I'm wild to hold the baby, zero in and coo—

to hold for a moment what's completely not mine. I give her a crust
of our fresh baked bread, warm from the oven, and miss the dinosaur sheets

on Brad's childhood bed, the must of that room and the wobbly lamp,
the *Rainbow Goblins* and sharp provolone cubes,

the Hershey bar stash, the overstuffed couch, the *struffoli*
dance, and the honey lacquer on that holiday dessert. I miss

the backgammon game I'll not play again against Uncle Mark—
how I knew to run instead of hit

but could never resist. He'd only roll doubles on Christmas Eve
and then again on Christmas Day. He'd win

afresh at Easter, take me out on the boat on the Fourth of July,
then unlatch what was his father's set

on turkey day—Brad's grandfather I never knew—
and build a backboard strong and walled, I almost always lost.

# DIVORCED BUSINESS PARTNER AIR TRAVEL

I interweave my fingers into Brad's palm
and knit a grip as the plane takes off.
It's a business trip, and we have to travel
together, our seats booked by the festival:
next to each other in the second row.
Brad knows how horribly I fly,
how my heart hiccups into arrhythmia
once I step through the threshold of steel
into air that smells of vacuum filters and stale
caffeine embers burnt into hot metal.
He knows I take a Xanax from its canister
as soon as I buckle down into the window.
He knows I take a second pill once the door
seals tight. I hear the captain's voice bellow
over the speaker like cold wind our wings
will fight to cut, landing in some other place
together. Brad sits next to me in that familiar
way of two bodies wrapped from a lifetime.
His shoulder remembers my temple—
no other place for my head to blunder,
I'm stoned over runway turf as we take off.
Brad's hand nurses my hand. Forearms
braided, my post-marriage gut wonders, warm
against the sea-salt creature of his tangles—
thick knot of curls I used to twirl—

# UNTITLED NOSTALGIA

We meet at the edge of the city to scatter our old cat's ashes,
I bring along the tiny conches we collected on honeymoon in Holbach.

Night was so humid thick there we did not touch.
Wrapped in mosquito netting, we slept, in fact, in separate beds.

He killed a leaflike bug—there, on our last morning, while we admired it,
by accident. Like so many things, we got too close.

Here we are now, on the edge of Manhattan with ashes & seashells in our hands
on the first sweet day of April as if nothing has passed—

as if we're walking to lunch along the pier, which is, in fact, what we do after.
I eat the fries off his plate, reach for the last sip of his iced tea—

After lunch, we walk to see the ducks, then stroll
through the spine of the Oculus sipping tea in to-go cups.

I've known him so well, it keeps surprising me to not know him anymore—
this version—somewhat familiar & completely a stranger—

Did I mention he didn't throw his shells into the river? Just the ashes.
I tell him, *It could've been like this*, walking around the city

eating lunch under the delightful sky, & he says, *Well,*
*we're doing that right now.*

# DAISY

She would've been five by now. First haircut strands Scotch-taped against a page
would've yellowed in the drawer.

I won't forget the scraping claw of end-of-marriage denouement—the rigor
of his cumming in a bed not ours. Harder than harpoon, his stare pushed in.

When he tore into the core of me, we made a decision. In, in he went,
and I let him—

There's no way two bodies tangle with such a lock
and not conceive.

I'd never had that sex before nor have I since; eyes blackholes of licorice,
he didn't really want to leave—put himself in me,

and in she swirled—to the melee. Socket flared—
then out with the melee—down the blackhole

of my pelvic flume, torn out
into no place we know.

# ANOTHER DIVORCED DAY AT THE RESTAURANT

We get ducks in for ragu like the old days. He cleaves
through their bones. I'm once again in the little room
pulling crumpled junk and dross from behind old
bottles of merlot. He likes to go through bone to feel
the knife hit the spot of white like a solid strike,
then knows to sever now requires body weight,
so he drives the heels of both his hands to separate

the bird. I'm not stuck to his skin with the dampness
of old wants. Those spiders creep back into the wine
room corners. I like to leave them, to leave
something alive in the aftermath, crack of duck
neck—how much to cleave in knot of hug
doesn't always mean two bodies
pressed and dear and wrapped again.

# FROM SMALL THING TO SMALL THING

I won't be divorced for another seven years when Mom buys a copy of *Stag's Leap* for my birthday the year it's released and inscribes it in tall, slanted loops of script—the way moms of that time looped their g's and their l's—

> 10/12
>
> Dear Maddy—
> You have made your own 'Stag'gering leap—
> I wish you success and happiness on your new path
>
> I Love You—
> Mom

My marriage is okay on the surface, yet, Mom puts this vital collection into my hands—I read it, and the poems strike some deep unconscious note about latent fractures that will stay with me until my marriage implodes.

The slim book lives on the shelf until its time to reemerge. Then, it becomes a primary companion, and I carry *Stag's Leap* around the city in my backpack. It's not only about reading it; it's about having it with me.

To be alone in a coffeeshop, and read these lines, "I am so ashamed / before my friends—to be known to be left / by the one who supposedly knew me best, / each hour is a room of shame"—I'm so ashamed, it gives me solace to have such companionship, to know someone else had come through it.

A year after the divorce, I meet Sharon Olds at Community of Writers, watch her walk into Lake Tahoe—the lake's freezing—everyone runs in and quickly out—she seems unaffected by the temperature. I see her from the shore—she doesn't rush, continues in until her shoulders slip under, her uncut shock of tresses mop the water white in a wake that reverberates from her body.

She signs my book:

> For Madeleine!
>
> Past present & future!
> xo
> Sharon
>
> June 2019

Then, she morphs the Knopf dog into a stag by drawing antlers from the pup's crown longer and taller than its whole body. At the bottom of the page, she draws mountain peaks and the lake.

When we meet for our 1:1 conference, I tell her how exhausted I feel writing about my marriage and divorce but that I can't seem to write about anything else. She tells me: *look at yourself, stop blaming him.* I've heard it from my dad, from my sister, my friends, my therapist, my other therapist, but this moment with her—I'm able to internalize it, to take it as the start of a way forward. *Write into the nouns!* she also tells me.

And so I do. I write *from small thing to small thing*—

# MARITAL OBJECTS, INVENTORY OF THINGS I KEEP

giant conch shell, Brad's last gift

the Oaxacan sculpture from our *luna de miel*—
    we wandered the markets for blue corn quesadillas stuffed with squash
    blossoms then spent the afternoons in bed where I read *Like Water for*
    *Chocolate* out loud.

trio of pictures from the paddleboat on the glacial lake in the wooden frame
    I burned so much, threw old gifts into the garbage, tied our vows
    to a branch near the labyrinth in Abiquiu—I hope I didn't burn those
    pictures. I burned his name in a bonfire, burned his name in another
    bonfire, burned pictures from a trip on the side of a westward road,
    I burned our sheets, dragged our mattress to the trash spot. Got a new
    one. Boiled a potion. Tossed seashells into the river.

    I smashed many mugs and plates—fortunately not the ones from
his mother's pastel earthenware set.
    I ate on those dishes last night.

I keep half the engagement diptych:
    the world in dots in a black universe
    with an aura heliotrope varnish
    in a thick line on canvas.

Some other things:

white ribbed bath sheet
    he used to wrap into after showers

two slate cheeseboards,
    another wedding gift

one periwinkle bowl,
    chipped

seven pieces of silverware:
    three forks and four butter knives

pictures from our first beach in fall
    Brad developed the image in the photo lab across from our dorms,
    slipped prints under my door

piece of yellow paper with a six-word note
    written twenty-two years ago, still folded—
    I know the sentence by heart.

## BRAD'S SOCKS, 1983

An envelope falls out as I pull *The Beauty of the Husband* from my bookshelf.

*Brad's Socks, 1983* in his mother's script. It's an envelope from his Dad's
stationery set with the Oakville Lane address embossed on the fold
in gold. I open it, and three remnants spill into my lap:

Brad's school picture from kindergarten: he's in a blue button-down
and striped tie against a midnight sky with pink lasers at obtuse
angles behind his back. A snippet of his hair from his first cut.
The crumbles of his first baby tooth.

I hold a little clump of blonde I no longer touch. He haunts.

# ENVELOPE OF HAIR AND TOOTH

I can't tuck it into the mail unadorned, anonymous, without explanation—
can you imagine his mother? Seventy-two, mid-morning: she reaches
into the mailbox at the edge of the driveway—little metal home full
of news, a bill to pay, something to do, or a card from one of the cousins.
She discovers the manila of my package larger than the rest with no return
address. Her name in my hand—her only guidepost. She opens it, her robe
closed against the morning, runs her fingers over the indentation of a golden
name embossed, slides her fingers over the letters—invocation of her once-
husband—she recognizes her own cursive: *Brad's Socks, 1983*—expects
two tokens of tiny blue with minute treads along the bottom like the traction
of goosebumps. Instead, she finds three souvenirs of Brad within. She holds
the parcel like a newborn. Her left hand cups the bottom of the packet;
her right hand presses the treasure deeper into her waffled cotton chest.
She's spooked as she cradles near the empty street of sparse maples
outside the home where nobody else lives anymore. At least she can set
the charms of hair and tooth and picture on her mantle—harbingers—
she can see them here: love the strands and sand of bone—her son.

# THE BEDROOM AT HIS MOTHER'S

I'm still in that room, that bundle
of dust, my cells, my decomposing
hair, my things in the broken bottom
drawer: albums from my birth, albums
from our early life—even a VHS
and sleeves of film—that's how far
we go back. Are they still there?
A coloring book, *One Hundred Years
of Solitude,* my striped beach throw
with the ribbon on its waist?
When Serena sleeps there, does she
ever open that very bottom dresser
drawer one morning while he sleeps—
and, looking for him find pieces
of me—picture of us on a paddle
boat, the poem I wrote for his mother
about baking together at Christmas,
tiny bottle of pink Bermuda sand?
Serena, if she finds me—does she open
and shake the small canister of sand
into her soft hands and let sand go?
I imagine her hands to be soft. Maybe
she just touches the sand; maybe
she puts some in her mouth.
I think she puts some in her mouth
to taste his past to ingest more history—
but she'll never hold our niece as a new-
born. She'll never be seen by his mother—
her vision's going—and she'll never know
his father. For he, too, is the sand.

# KNIFE SKILLS

I make a remarkable breakfast burrito—Brad taught me the ratio
of hot sauce to eggs, how to chop in chicken sausage and cheese.
He taught me the tradition of how a chef takes care of their knife—
my once-husband—watching him at the restaurant: choke up
on the handle, rowboat chop, make sure to scrape with the back
of the knife so as not to dull the blade's finesse—

when we move out of our apartment, he leaves me to pack first.
So I move through kitchen drawers; my fingers comb over utensils,
sharp artifacts from culinary school and remnants from our registry.
Like in a sunken ship, there's time—things scattered and washed
over the drawer's basin. I don't take much, for so much of it isn't
mine: the spoons or graters, spatula, peeler, measuring cups—our
lives measured by what we will or will not take. I let my eyes glide
over his knives, tempted. Leave them.

I ask him to shop with me to buy my own. He never says no anymore,
except makes clear he's not coming back. Then, like so many times,
I find myself with him again as he walks with me around a store—
a homewares store. Everything is how it is. We're in our winter coats,
and when a clerk opens the case, we lean in. I pick a Wüsthof: heavy,
classic. I buy it. I've been loyal to this wooden-handled blade—still
have it, the only knife I need.

I like to think Brad would like to know I still chop well, I sharpen,
and I take decent care of my knife. He'd like to know it's clean,
tucked into its sleeve three drawers down to the right of the stove.

# DEBT

I hadn't heard good thunder in ages.

Brad said, *I'm leaving*—
he's prone to bloody noses

when the rain comes. When we met,
I already knew the look on his face

meant our girl got lifted above him
from my body. She wasn't.

I loved him like the wire-flower
sculpture with tiny, yellow stamens.

No light for a long time, no sun—
in the afternoon, a sliver. We'd wait

for it together, tap the other: *Look!*
*The star is on the floor.*

In part, that's why he stayed a bit—
to wiggle his toes in the sunsplash

and smile at the upheaval.

# [YEARS LATER] BRAD BECOMES A FATHER

buzz of text—
I'm one of the first
to know, of course

# [YEARS LATER] BRAD BECOMES A FATHER #2

Congrats

I write back—
preprogrammed confetti
showers the screen

# [YEARS LATER] BRAD BECOMES A FATHER #3

When Brad met his son, when he looked into those eyes,
did who we didn't have live for a moment?
How could she have not? She landed just for a pause

to wave hello as a last chance for two people to survive
an exhausted, mythologized tale. Brad's new one, ready
for this world: I hope he may be happy. He's not mine.
That makes me happy. My friend—

no one would've been happy
had I made the choice to keep those ropes
tied to the sinking boats of each other..

# [YEARS LATER] BRAD BECOMES A FATHER #4

Still business partners, I buy Brad a baby gift:
matching shirt-set for him and baby to share.

I know his size, of course—I was his wife—
jersey cotton tee silk-screened with a pea-pod

—one pea missing.
On the onesie: the pea!

I'm astonished at my ability to not be wretched
and jealous—and I love holding babies—when

will I cross paths with his new creature?
Will I be able to ignore the heavy head asleep

on his collarbone? Will I bump into Brad
at the restaurant and hold the door open

for his stroller? She would've been just shy
of six by now, chewing crust in his lap.

# FACT CHECK

I'm not exactly sure the type of street food we ate in the plaza near our hotel on our honeymoon, so I call Brad.

He reminds me, *the tortillas were blue corn and not flour.* Reminds me we grinned as the squash blossoms wilted in the heat and the *queso Oaxaca* crisped around the edges like our tanned and freckled noses.

He has to hang up quickly—I hear baby noise in the background. No need for us to have a long goodbye anymore.

*Mad,* he says, *I've got to run,* and hangs up before the syllable of *Bye* leaves my lips.

I switch to text:

> Thank you!
> I've been on a writing tear

Like what

> Just reflecting on life, marriage, old chapter new chapter, how we mended our relationship finally

I agree

> And it's got me feeling sentimental, thoughtful

> Incredibly bittersweet—beautiful to get here—somehow we got through the most awful destruction and there's still love to have kinship now, and that's a lot of what I'm writing through

He gives the heart reply.

> I find it all very ironic because we are also better suited to be with who we are each with now

I know

We text a little more about the restaurant, how our lives changed.

I've been in the archives this whole week, and I'm perusing old work as we go back and forth.

I stumble upon a poem I wrote in his grandma's voice about her wedding. I sat with her at the card table in the living room at his mother's house one afternoon, asked her questions about the day, and transcribed her answers:

> *We had demitasse coffee with dessert. The cups were white with gold around the rim. It was Italian coffee. We ate pastries and cake. But that was 1942, a long time ago. I looked sad at the wedding. We took serious pictures back then.*

I share the poem with Brad.

> I sent you a poem I just found btw
>
> It's not a poem poem but it's your grandma talking and me taking notes

I just read it

It's great

I give the heart reply.

We text a little more. I send him a picture of my kitten walking across the kitchen table. I just bought chairs like the ones we used to eat lunch on in our damp bathing suits at his aunt and uncle's house at the beach.

I loved that pool and those chairs.

We'd swum at that house three days before he packed his little green duffle bag and left. I dove in and out of the deep end while he listened to a podcast on the other side of the deck.

I'm writing about objects I've cherished: a picture he took on the beach, the note he pulled out of his pocket one morning, early on at breakfast on campus, as I dipped French toast sticks into syrup.

I text him a bit of the piece in progress.

> Here's a snippet.
> [blushing emoji]

Oooh those French toast stix

THAT'S WHAT YOU TOOK FROM
THIS? [face plant emoji]

Well it was the only thing I forgot.

# THE BIG COUCHES

It was partially open, the family-size Hershey's Bar, sitting on the counter at Brad's Dad's house, next to an ordinary ceramic bowl, milk-colored round thing perfect for holding the chocolate portions Brad's Dad snapped off for Grandma, who lived upstairs in Brad's Dad's house, who liked me most, because I was the only girlfriend or wife of Brad's she knew before she died, because I was a member of that family for 16 years, from 19 on up to 35, and I grew up visiting that house, upstate.

Today, I took a nap on the new couch that was finally delivered to my new home in my new life with a husband who isn't Brad. I didn't know when I married the first time that a vow has nothing to do with permanence. Words hold nothing without actions that align with their meaning, like saying I took a nap without telling you the way my mind wandered.

In the dream, which is really a recollection, I wondered if I've ever been more comfortable than the night Brad and I fell asleep on the floor in front of his Grandma's couches in front of the fire. The longer the fire held, the deeper a balm it became. We were too close; it was too hot on our faces, yet we seemed to sleep better, maybe from the smoke.

The couches were comically oversized for the room. And it was a big living room—his Dad lived in a large Victorian at the top of a hill with a frog that lived in a pond in the yard—when I think of the Bashō kerplunk, I think of that frog pond, how that night in front of the couches was the sleepiest I've ever been, and also the most peaceful right below the surface of something.

We had, after all, been drinking whatever old bottle of cream sherry sat in the kitchen near the stack of oversized Hershey's Bars Brad's Dad bought in bulk on visits to Target.

We'd hotboxed the bathroom shower—we were only college kids back then visiting for the weekend—what else was there to do? We'd had the kind of sex where clothes wound up all over the floor, and I'm sure we were louder than respectful—if I yelled too loud when we'd been fucking, Brad's Grandma never seemed to mind.

She sustained on a specific diet: those Hershey's bars broken into pieces in the little bowl, boxes of mini powdered sugared donuts, and cubes of Havarti with dill. We'd eat spaghetti with *braciole* or roast turkey and

Yorkshire pudding, which never quite rose right, and she'd sit adjacent to her sweets and the savory cheese and talk to us through a ring of confectioner's sugar around her lips.

Then, we'd lounge around on those couches sipping the cream sherry—there were two of them, relics from some magnificent room in Grandma's mansion in the backcountry of New England, a room that required furniture of this scale, upholstered plush with embroidered flowers.

Here, they were wedged in an L-shape butting up to each other—and the walls of the room just to fit—and because of their tremendousness, we shrank into a more childlike state, supinating and rolling around in pajamas by sundown, tickling, giggling, falling asleep on our bellies on the floor.

I don't think we ever fought in that house. Just drank the cream sherry and smoked joints in the shower, ate pasta and meat, and then chocolate that wasn't Grandma's—usually a box with fancy truffles Brad's Dad had stowed away for the special occasion of my sweet tooth on our visits.

We slept with wonder. It never occurred to us we would ever sleep next to anyone else than each other. I've only remembered any of this since I sunk into the pillows yesterday, on my new couch, fantastic, like clouds.

# AUBADE FOR FORTY

He's the first to text me, Happy fortieth—my ex-husband. Dawn
where he wakes with his kiddo and also remembers

this is the first decade he's not the one whispering to a waiter
to put a candle in dessert—*the most chocolatey one*—my new

husband will say tonight while we eat lobster
in cream sauce, feeding each other shoestring french fries

while Brad changes a diaper a time zone away.

# NOTES

"Prologue: Breakfast Date with My Ex-Husband" references the snow angel in Ocean Vuong's poem "Snow Theory."

The title "From Small Thing to Small Thing" is a line from "While He Told Me" and contains a line quoted from "Known to be Left," both by Sharon Olds.

"Bury It" borrows its title from *Bury It* by Sam Sax.

"The Big Couches" references Allen Ginsberg's translation "Frog Haiku" by Matsuo Bashō.

# PUBLICATION ACKNOWLEDGMENTS

Thank you to the following journals that published these poems, many in earlier versions:

| | |
|---|---|
| *armarolla* | Prologue: Breakfast Date with My Ex-Husband (as "I Collect a Box of My Old Journals from His Mother's House") |
| *Neologism* | When We Open the Restaurant |
| | New Routine (as "Schism") |
| | After Drafting the Divorce Agreement |
| *Bell Ombre* | Fried Baby Artichokes |
| *Mount Hope Magazine* | Knife Skills (as "Skill from My Marriage") |
| | Nothing Has Ever Taken Him Further Away from Me (as "Starting to Part") |
| | One Night Early On (as "One Night Early on at the Restaurant") |
| | Divorced Business Partner Family Reunion (as "Divorced Business Partners") |
| *The Virginia Normal* | The Bedroom at His Mother's |
| | Going to the Bathroom in Central Booking |
| | Out to Dinner with My Husband When We Are Separated |
| *Palette Poetry* | Cellular Parting & The Last Time (as "Confession") |
| *Apricity Magazine* | Divorced Business Partner Meeting (as "Ex-Husband-Business-Partner-Meeting") |
| *Belletrist Magazine* | Another Divorced Day at the Restaurant |
| *Visitant* | [Years Later] Brad Becomes a Father #3 |

# ACKNOWLEDGMENTS

How can I even begin to capture my gratitude for a life full of incredible people? In no way is this list wholly inclusive.

Thank you to the entire team at Howling Bird Press for believing in and helping me bring this book to life. And to Chloe Mata Crane and the Baltz team for shining light onto this little dream.

Thank you to the creative writing programs and conferences, full of talented facilitators and peers, that have supported my growth as a poet: Community of Writers, Napa Valley Writer's Conference, Roger Williams University, Brooklyn College, and the SF Creative Writing Institute.

Thank you to my many formative teachers: Joyce Berrian, Meg Schaefer, Adam Braver, Jerry Williams, Délana Dameron, Hollie Hardy, and Mirabai Starr. Thank you to Mark Doty—finding my way to study with you has been, and continues to be, an absolute gift.

Thank you to my peers from various workshop groups who have read and helped shape many of the poems in this book, especially: Lo Naylor, Mary Walsh, Tanya Thurman, Melissa Anderson, Melissa Christine Goodrum, Ed Go, Noah Grossman, and Michael Whalen.

Thank you to my dear friends who held me up while going through the process: Frank Wildermann, Gianna Gioia, Lara Storm, Ben Swire, Jaime Grechika, Samantha Story, Kayte Ringer, my sweet Quinn and Phoebe, and the Juniper yoga community.

Thank you to my family: Doon, Scott, Dad, Aunt Margo, and Mom—here in spirit—my first editor and biggest champion.

Thank you to my mentor, Genine Lentine—and her sidekick, Jesse. Genine, you have held a space for me to grow and learn that has changed the course of my life and career. I'm lucky to get to spend my days deep in revision with you.

Thank you to Wheelie, Rosie, and Nellie for always sitting on my lap as I write.

And, of course, to my dear Jeffrey—thank you for being by my side as I continue along this path. I love you for eternity.

Emily Hyland's poetry has appeared in *The Brooklyn Review*, *Frontier Poetry*, and *The Hollins Critic*, among others. She earned her MFA in poetry and her MA in English education from Brooklyn College. Her cookbook, *Emily: The Cookbook*, was published by Ballantine Books, an imprint of Random House, in 2018. Hyland is the eponymous co-founder of the international restaurant groups Pizza Loves Emily + Emmy Squared Pizza. She lives in Santa Fe, New Mexico, where she writes and teaches yoga. emilyhyland.com / emmysquaredpizza.com / pizzalovesemily.com

# ABOUT HOWLING BIRD PRESS

Howling Bird Press is the book imprint of Augsburg's MFA in Creative Writing program. Students enrolled in the MFA's publishing concentration, a two-semester course sequence, do the work of running the press, including editing, marketing, and fundraising, while studying the publishing profession and the book trade. The press sponsors an annual nationwide contest, judged by the students enrolled in the publishing concentration and senior faculty of the Creative Writing program, and publishes the winning manuscript. The author receives a cash prize, book publication, nationwide distribution, and an invitation to read at the MFA in Creative Writing's summer residency in Minneapolis. The contest is open to manuscripts of poetry, fiction, and nonfiction on an alternating basis.

Howling Bird Press wishes to acknowledge our editors Chilah Brown, Pamela Morgan, Phyrne Nelson, Alison Summer, Brent Weaver. We also thank Augsburg's MFA faculty and mentors, including MFA director Lindsay Starck, Stephan Clark, Alice Eve Cohen, Anika Fajardo, Andy Froemke, Michael Kleber-Diggs, Carson Kreitzer. We thank English Department co-chairs Stephan Clark and Dal Liddle and Augsburg president Paul Pribbenow. Special thanks to the supporters of the Howling Bird Press Publishing Fund, who—through Augsburg's Give to the Max campaign—provided generous support, including Cass Dalglish (in memory of Louis Carroll Branca), Kay Malchow, and many more donors.

Previous prize winners:
*At the Border of Wilshire & Nobody* by Marci Vogel, 2015, Poetry
*The Topless Widow of Herkimer Street* by Jacob M. Appel, 2016, Fiction
*Still Life with Horses* by Jean Harper, 2017, Nonfiction
*Simples* by KateLynn Hibbard, 2018, Poetry
*Irreversible Things* by Lisa Van Orman Hadley, 2019, Fiction
*Self, Divided* by John Medeiros, 2020, Nonfiction
*The Second Longest Day of the Year* by Jean Prockott, 2021, Poetry
*I Have Her Memories Now* by Carrie Grinstead, 2022, Fiction
*Boolean Logic* by Morgan Christie, 2023, Nonfiction